MW00533035

Coming From Behind the Curtain: 7 Steps to…Revealing the True Essence of YOU!

ISBN 978-1-54391-907-3

Printed in the USA by BookBaby

Acknowledgement & Dedication

I want to first acknowledge my Lord Jesus Christ and all his phenomenal glory. He has blessed me beyond measure and greater than anything I could have ever imagined. He has poured his undying favor over my life; his insurmountable love for me is beyond my own comprehension. For his love and faithfulness, I am truly grateful! Secondly, I would like to acknowledge my friend and Development Editor, Ms. Tiffany Brown, for her support in this process.

This Book is Lovingly Dedicated to...

My Parents: William & Brenda Chaney

You are first my parents, but you are also my spiritual support system. Thanks for believing in me even as a young child who had so many dreams and talents. You provided the opportunity to travel from state to state, participate in homecoming courts, talent shows, modeling agencies, acting, and many more enriching activities throughout my life. Having God in the forefront of our home provided balance in our lives that would sustain me in everything I would do even today. You both inspired me to have my own relationship with Jesus Christ.

Thank you for instilling in me a strong sense of push to never settle and be complicit in life but rather to always reach for greater heights. Your love, faith, friendship, and your kind, gentle spirit makes living with you in my life each day a gift. I would not be the woman I am today without the seeds you have sown in my life. I respect you, love you, admire you, and look forward to spending the rest of our lives together. Thank you for being the best parents that God could have possibly blessed me with, and most importantly, thanks for being *true*!

My Children: Janae & John

My sweet, beautiful, and loving children . . . You both have been my inspiration the minute I found out I was pregnant. Your unconditional love for me has given me the heart to continue to be the best example that I can be to exhibit love to you both. When I look in both your eyes, it gives me so much strength and faith to keep winning. Thank you for being such an influence of love and support for Mommy. I love you both more than you could ever know!

My Siblings: Tony, Willetta, & Meloniese

I appreciate your love and support over the years. Our talks strengthened me, your protection comforted me, your wisdom inspired me, and your love sustained me. I appreciate you each in a special way. We have an unbreakable bond thanks to the love our parents showed us. I am honored to call you sister and brother. I love you!

My Extended Family: Mother Dorothy Dukes & the Late Superintendent Horace Dukes

Thank you for being great examples of what the Word of God is and what the Word of God looks like in teaching me the fundamentals of Christianity. Your impact in my life is immeasurable and so is my love for you.

My Grandmother: Pearlene Glass-Tanks

Last but not least, I must thank my beloved grandmother who is no longer here in the natural, but in spirit; you have never left me. Your strong faith in God has always shone brightly even as I was a child growing into adulthood. Your sincere prayers and words of wisdom will always be in my heart. You are deeply missed but never forgotten. Love you, grandmother!

Table of Contents

Foreword By: Juandolyn Stokes

To know Jarneen is to love her! Her passion for uplifting and serving others is obvious upon first meeting her. Watching her grace and beauty as she engages with others is genuine and simply amazing. The smile, the success, and her undying faith have not come without struggle. Jarneen has made a concerted effort to move past the struggles to embrace her best self. In doing so, she has been able to inspire all of us who have the distinct pleasure of knowing her.

As I read the first draft of this book, I was encouraged by the wisdom, hope, and adaptable strategies she shares. Reading this book will be a decision you won't regret. Be blessed and be prepared to grow throughout this journey!

Jarneen,
This book is a blessing!

Thank you

From the bottom of my heart!
Juandolyn Stokes

Foreword By: Tiffany Brown

I am so proud of my sister in Christ and friend, Jarneen Chaney! I had the distinct pleasure of walking with her as she masterfully drafted this guide. I can personally attest to the care, devotion, and heart that she put into every word. Her wonderfully scripted stories help us all see bits of ourselves while gaining a better understanding of others.

As you will see, this message is a gift from God meant to inspire you and reaffirm his word in your life. Jarneen eloquently writes from a place of wisdom, experience, and victory. She boldly speaks out on subjects that many of us hide from daily. Through her words and stories, I have been blessed and encouraged to effect immediate change in my life. I am working daily to implement her recommended strategies as I strive to change the landscape of my life. It is no coincidence that Jarneen would have me serve as her *Development Editor* on this project. God knows that being close to her and close to this amazing project has been a life-changing experience for me!

Jarneen....Thank you for your heart and obedience. You are truly helping others live a better and more fulfilling life! I love you, my sister!

Tiffany B.

Introduction

This is the memoir of a mother, a former wife, an actor, and a business owner who has unrepentantly chosen to come from behind her CURTAIN, shining a spotlight on her own past experiences to help readers walk in their purpose!

Are You Ready for Your Debut?

Some may ask what coming from behind the curtain means and how it relates to my life and the choices I make daily. Let's first take a moment to define the term *Coming from Behind the Curtain* in its figurative meaning. We will then take a journey together as we reflect on our past and the life that we are currently living.

Coming from Behind the Curtain...Let me make a comparison to one of my greatest loves, theater. In theater, a curtain is used to cleverly mask what's really on stage. When you enter the auditorium, you enter this magical space filled with the expectation of what's to come when the curtain is opened. The curtain is thick, usually velvet, and visually appealing to the eye. Of course, it has to be. Why? This curtain has to deflect attention away from the set positioned just behind the curtain. It is used to hide the set, props, actors, and all things not meant to be seen until the perfect time. In life, many of us spend time hiding behind the curtain as we work to get things perfectly situated behind it. As long as the curtain is up and hiding my *life's stage*, I can work through my issues and act in secrecy. Thank you curtain!

When the ropes are pulled back and the curtain starts to open, the audience is exposed to the real set—in this case, real life. The concept of *Coming from Behind the Curtain* speaks to the brave heart who is ready, willing, and able to do the necessary work backstage (our lives) to present a beautiful creation, the masterpiece of who you really are, so you can discover the true essence of you.

Now, let's take a moment to do some introspective thinking by examining some of our relationships: familial, romantic, and platonic (all relationships). Ask yourself three important questions.

1. What have you hidden from so long that you have become numb to it?
2. How have you dealt with this issue?
3. Do you sweep these issues under the imaginary rug, just to put on the *perfect face* before the curtain opens for the show?

There are many of us who have intentionally decided to hide from the world of weird looks, failures, pride, low self-esteem, doubt, loss of material things, self-value, respect, and insecurities in an effort to protect ourselves and our image. Let's make a personal assessment by asking yourself the following:

1. How do I overcome these past issues to prevent myself from making the same mistakes?
2. Have I become complacent with just settling because of my own fear of failure?

I have asked myself these very questions. I have struggled with the inability to break away from unhealthy situations, knowing that I deserved better. By better, I mean the way I was treated by people and also what had become unhealthy norms in my life. I was trapped in a life of *settling*. One personal example is with my past relationships. I had been married twice, with each marriage being totally different, yet I still considered each a complete failure. I often told myself that I needed to leave . . . just break up, move on, and divorce! Then I talked myself into staying. I felt the need to recondition myself and learn to stay. Staying in my mind meant just dealing with it and being quiet, believing that God would single-handedly fight my battle, even when I knew that my husband wasn't doing his part.

As I was writing this book, I was thinking about the best way to talk to men and women about the choices we make in our lives. We all want to make the right choice, but we sometimes struggle getting to this point. I discovered that you only reach this point when you're ready to seriously pray for change. This is not a one-time prayer. It is a prayer that must be consistent and steadfast. You must be honest while crying out to your Father. I make a habit of asking God to have his way in my life and to make me comfortable with the subsequent change.

Now friends, when you pray fervently for change, be prepared for it. Trust me, God can and will erase the scars, past disappointments, and disloyalty you've experienced, as well as the disrespect that has plagued your relationships. He then begins to do a new work in you and in your heart. What you must do is allow the gift of the Holy Spirit to govern and abide within you so that you can receive healing and wholeness. At this point, your heart will begin to mend itself back together again. The wonderful thing about the process is that once you can begin to look at yourself, God will show you who you really are, if you are willing to do the work. He will let you know that you are the apple of his eye and that he only wants to love you and help you live your best life!

Each step outlined in the process will begin with a personal account of stories from family, friends, and myself to help illustrate the very essence and main points of each action item. These stories are true and created to help you identify with others who have similar stories.

Each step ends with an opportunity to self-reflect and do some work. The note section should be used to help mark your progress. You must be diligent in this process in order to see real change in your life!

Happy reading! Sit back, relax, and let's begin this beautiful journey together!

With Love,

Jarneen

STEP 1: Self-Evaluation

As I prepared to present this chapter on self-evaluation, I was reminded of a conversation I had with a dear friend. She had reached that broken place that so many of us can identify within our own lives. She was seeking answers in hopes of regaining control of her life, her livelihood, and overall emotional and spiritual health. Walk through Tiffany's journey with me. I'm sure you can relate!

Tiffany's Story

God gave Tiffany the gift of being a woman who truly knows how to love unconditionally. He gave her the gift of forever *to bestow upon others. In this, I mean that he gave her the heart to be* ride-or-die *for those she loves and calls close friends/family. Her trait is to always be very helpful to others, but in all honesty, this was sometimes detrimental to herself. When I say Tiffany, I might just be talking to you too.*

I know Tiffany well. She is an analytical person who can systematically dismantle any situation to find a solution to a problem. What she didn't realize is that, in some cases, she was more of a reactionary analytical thinker. She ran heart-first, mind-last into platonic, familial, and romantic partnerships. Please don't take the use of partnership literally as it was the opposite many times. Tiffany selflessly used her analytical, unconditionally loving, and ride-or-die *giving skills for others at the drop of a dime, with no thought about it. Why was this the case?*

Well, God showed her why . . . You see, her mother married the first man she ever dated when she was twelve. It was different, but she was hopeful. He had to be great because her mom was happy and he was a minister. They were going to start their own ministry together! Then about 6 months in, Tiffany and her mother learned that he was addicted to crack and life forever changed. Through theft, lies, betrayal, and emotional abuse, Tiffany stood with her mom. She physically and emotionally fought her battles because she was the only child left in the house. Her older brother was then living in New Jersey. Tiffany decided to act as a savior and protector of the one person who meant the most to her, her mom. So, she was that to her, but she was also an honor roll student, a cheerleader, and a little socialite. Tiffany matured quickly. Her mom could only trust Tiffany with her truth, so Tiffany quickly perfected a gift given to her by God— being faithful and steadfast, always giving to those she loved. To this day, she expresses no regrets because she was her mom and she deserved that and more.

Fast forward to today and Tiffany is still the ride-or-die friend, sister, daughter, girlfriend, etc. This is a good thing when shared with the right person and right situation. The problem is that Tiffany gave this same devotion, as she conditioned herself to do with her mom, to a few too many people that didn't deserve it, so much so that she almost let her own well run dry.

In closing, I say this to you . . . Continue to be the beautiful person God gifted you to be, just like Tiffany did. Just be sure you take time to assess these gifts, how you're using them, and why you use them the way you do. It took prayer and quiet time to learn why Tiffany went so hard for people, many times to her own detriment. Well, it's because she conditioned herself to do this at the age of twelve. She eventually changed her perspective and now knows how to accept and cherish this gift, while also preserving it for God-ordained partners, friendships, and familial and romantic relationships.

It's Time for Some Self-Evaluation

When you think of the word self-evaluation, what comes to your mind? Self-evaluation is defined as a process or an instance of assessing oneself and one's achievement (SWOT Analysis, 2014). One's ability to engage in self-examination can positively influence his or her relationship with others in their development and overall learning process. Okay, let's just sit and really think about the last time you took a look in the mirror to truly examine who you are and what makes you act in positive and negative ways. Think about it.

1. What makes you tick?

3

2. What are some of your biggest successes and failures?

3. What led you to these successes and failures?

Self-evaluation is a critical component to growth and achieving your best version of YOU! Without self-evaluation, you are bound to repeat mistakes and miss opportunities. You limit your growth potential and stifle your true gifts and talents. If you take the time to truly evaluate yourself, the good and the bad, you will at least know where you stand and can effect a positive change in your life.

Let's go deeper here. Many of us struggle every day facing that big giant we call SELF. If you can really be honest when you look at the reflection called *you*, then and only then can change begin to take its full course. I have often found out that if you can be honest with yourself and the reality that we all have issues and shortcomings, transformation can begin. In relationships, be it with your husband, wife, sister, brother, or a co-worker, if you have been known for failed relationships or people just so happen to leave you, you have to realize that you might just be the issue. Not everyone is

4

wrong. We all have issues. Believe it or not, some more than others. When you come to the realization that only God can help you out when those difficult challenges arise in your life, then true healing can begin. Not only will God show you how to deal with *yourself* and your life, but he will also show you how to overcome these challenges successfully. Now that God has your attention in providing a way of deliverance, it's only fair to share it with others to create a healthy *you*. Let's begin to walk in full abundance that he has so proudly provided for you. Self-evaluation is a necessary anecdote to a successful inner being.

In the spirit of walking in full abundance, I would like to suggest that we employ a method used by many professionals to assess a business' viability, in hopes of seeing growth and sustainability. This evaluation tool is called SWOT Analysis. SWOT stands for "Strengths, Weaknesses, Opportunities, and Threats" in an organization (SWOT Analysis, 2014). A SWOT analysis is used in the early stages of strategic planning, in problem-solving, and decision making, or for making staff aware of the need for change (SWOT Analysis, 2014). The SWOT Analysis can be used at a personal level, so let's do just that.

5

Please take a moment and walk through this challenge with me. For each letter, there is an associated word. Please record the items with the corresponding letter. For example, as mentioned, *W* is for Weaknesses. I would list mounting financial responsibility as a weakness for me in attaining my goals and life's true purpose. So here we go, LET'S WRITE!

List the *Strengths, Weaknesses, Opportunities,* and *Threats* that could keep you behind the CURTAIN, making it difficult to discover the true essence of yourself. Be honest in your assessment. Write openly about the positive and negative things that you see currently in your life.

S Strengths	W Weaknesses
O Opportunities	T Threats

S.W.O.T Analysis

Strengths

Things to think about....

- What advantages do you have?
- What do you do better than anyone else?
- What unique resources can you draw upon?

_____

_____

_____

_____

_____

_____

_____

_____

_____

_____

Weaknesses

Things to think about....

- What could you improve?
- What should you avoid?
- What do people around you see as your weaknesses?

_____

_____

_____

_____

_____

_____

_____

_____

_____

_____

_____

_____

Opportunities

Things to think about....

- What good opportunities can you spot?
- What interesting trends are you aware of?
- What changes can you see in your life regarding social patterns, population profiles, lifestyle changes, and so on.

_____

_____

_____

_____

_____

_____

_____

_____

_____

_____

_____

Threats

Things to think about....

- What obstacles do you face?
- Do you have bad debt or cash-flow problems?
- Could any of your weaknesses seriously threaten your livelihood?

_____

_____

_____

_____

_____

_____

_____

_____

_____

_____

_____

Reference:

SWOT analysis. (2014). In Qatar Financial Center, & Qatar Financial Center (Eds.), *QFinance: the ultimate resource*. London, UK: A&C Black.

Notes & Reflections

Now that we've explored this chapter together, it's time for you to spread your wings and fly, butterfly. Use the space provided to record your notes, major takeaways, and your plan of action for moving forward. Be honest and bold! Use this quiet time to invest in YOU!

_____

_____

_____

_____

_____

_____

_____

_____

_____

_____

_____

STEP 2: Focus on Assessing Your Level of Pain & Hurt

The subject of pain can be a very touchy matter. Many of us don't even want to acknowledge pain or do the work to assess where our pain is coming from in our lives. Let's look at Tasha's story.

Tasha's Story

Tasha married the man of her dreams. He met all the points on her checklist. Even though she loved him, there seemed to be an uncomfortable disconnect between the two of them. One obvious problem was Tasha's insecurity. She worked hard to control it, but she always felt uneasy and unsure in the relationship no matter how hard her husband tried to convince her otherwise.

This problem led to larger problems in the marriage, eventually causing a separation. Tasha did not want to give up on her marriage, so she sought counseling. Through her discovery process, she learned that issues that she had with her father were eroding her relationship. Her father left home when she was two, never to return. Not only was he absent from their home, but he was also totally absent from her life. She subsequently developed abandonment issues that would haunt her in every relationship.

Tasha was hurt by her father. Instead of being able to identify the hurt and seek God for healing, she simply buried the pain. When she finally fell in love, she became nervous that her husband would abandon her like her father did. She projected her pain and hurt onto her husband, unintentionally creating a toxic environment.

After discovering her pain, she was able to work through her issues. She eventually invited her husband to counseling with her, and by the Grace of God, they were able to repair what had seemingly been broken.

Hurt People, Hurt People

So often we hear the saying that hurt people, hurt people. It's true, isn't it? All of us have been hurt by people who were hurt by other hurt people. When I use the word hurt, I mean in actions, words, and attitudes that are intentional or unintentional. Hurt can manifest in different forms of mental, physical, and emotional abuse. It doesn't matter what form it's displayed in; it still hurts. When you first meet someone, you can't look at him or her and determine what hurt looks like in them. When people try to

14

function in areas of a relationship where they have unhealed hurts, they inevitably hurt others, even if they love them. Most of the hurt people experience stems from a lack of a relationship with their mother or father. As much as we mature in our lives, past hurts always come back to haunt us if forgiveness hasn't occurred.

Yes, it can hurt if a father abandoned his son or daughter. It definitely hurts when a mother spends the majority of her time in the clubs or with a bottle in her hand. Some suffer from the hurt of never meeting their biological father. That pain can fester, and that's when the enemy begins to speak to the mind and create suggestions that something is wrong with you. He can whisper those devilish nothings in your ear saying "If only mom or dad wanted me, instead of trying to abort me..." or "If only my mom had figured out how to improve her relationships with men so that I could have seen what a healthy family looked like and I wouldn't be in this situation...."

We all know the saying "The devil is a liar." Those thoughts he infects you with are meant to cause you harm,

15

just like an infectious disease. This is when you have to cast out those voices and not focus on the hurt others caused but the promises God had made instead. You must change your confessions. Step 6 will discuss this in greater detail, but it's all about changing your mindset so that real change can occur in your life.

Uprooting negative seeds of hurt and replacing them with seeds of forgiveness is the best way to be healed from your hurt, preventing you from passing on hurt to those you love. If these issues are not resolved with the help of Jesus Christ and a strong family support system, you are looking at an emotional bomb just waiting to happen. We, as believers, must heal our bleeding hearts before entering into new relationships. If we are not healed completely, we can operate out of hurt, and any advice that you might have for a friend could come out of your past hurt. This continues the spread of that infectious disease.

So, how do we know when we have reached the place of healing and can truly function from an emotionally healthy place? There are a few key concepts to assess when making this determination. Moving forward, it is critical that you walk yourself through these questions to engage in healthy relationships. Examine your level of pain and hurt by asking yourself the following and answering honestly:

- *Am I emotionally responsible?*

This is when you take full responsibility for your life and your actions. You no longer blame mama, daddy, the devil, or anyone else for your pain, hurt, or emotional state. You stop saying "You make me so mad when you do that," and replace that language with "I feel mad when you do that because..."

- *Am I emotionally honest?*

When you are truly healed from the hurt and pain, you start to know and own your feelings. This is a necessary step to self-acceptance and self-understanding. You can then accept yourself with all the bumps and bruises and recover.

- *Am I emotionally open?*

Are you able to share your feelings with people in an appropriate manner and at appropriate times? At this point, you have learned the value of venting feelings to let feelings go and also the dangers involved in hiding feelings.

- *Am I emotionally assertive?*

An emotionally assertive person knows how to express themselves and is to be able to ask for and to receive the nurturing that they need and want, first from self, and then from others. They assert their emotional needs in all of their relationships, to create an emotional balance.

- *Do I have emotional understanding?*

If you can honestly answer yes to this question, then you can understand the actual cause-and-effect processes of emotional responsibility and emotional irresponsibility.

- *Am I emotionally detached?*

At this point, you live without the burden and snare of self-concepts, self-images, self-constructs, group concepts, and thing concepts. Not having self-concepts to defend or promote, you can remain unaffected by the *blame game* and the projections of hurt people that will intentionally or unintentionally cause you pain.

Notes & Reflections

Now that we've explored this chapter together, it's time for you to spread your wings and fly, butterfly. Use the space provided to record your notes, major takeaways, and your plan of action for moving forward. Be honest and bold! Use this quiet time to invest in YOU! Assess your level of pain so that God can provide your perfect cure!

_____

_____

_____

_____

_____

_____

_____

_____

_____

STEP 3: Examine Your Wants Versus His Will for Your Life

This chapter really hits home for me, and I'm sure it will hit home for most of you. A friend inspired this chapter as we spoke candidly about our own experiences. This friend shared a story with me and gave me permission to share it with you. Does any of this sound familiar?

Mark's Story

Mark is definitely one of the good guys. After a few failed relationships, he was left to wonder if there were really any good women left out there for him. He's definitely a guy that would get many women's attention, but he was very selective in deciding whom to pursue.

Now, here's the catch: this was not always the case. Mark was the typical man chasing beauty over character and spirit. He wanted an arm piece so that no one could deny her beauty and his swag. He only wanted women who would help elevate his social status, often ignoring the parts of her that really mattered, well past the physical.

His last relationship helped him see the error of his ways. He had caught the baddest fish in the sea. She definitely got attention from men every time they stepped out. She was so used to getting attention, she began to crave it like

our bodies should crave water. She sought attention by any means necessary, often disrespecting Mark in the process. He became really upset with the lack of respect she showed him. After all, he was doing everything she wanted—paying bills, taking her out, and buying nice things. Why couldn't this woman just act right? Well, Mark began to really dissect the person he now called his mate.

After much evaluation, it was difficult for him to pull out the Godly characteristics he was raised to seek out in a mate. He would literally hear his mama advise him of the pitfalls set to entrap men who failed to seek God's best— his will. He was shameful to see himself in such a shallow and petty place. He put so much emphasis on what he thought he wanted in his FINE mate that the essence and true character of the woman was no longer even a thought.

Finally, after two years of heading nowhere, Mark was able to truly assess his missteps and end the damaging relationship. Mark's focus now is to simply wait, strengthen his expectations of a Godly union, and allow his heavenly father to have his will. His prayer now is "God have your will and give me the peace to be okay with it."

Friends, are you fed up yet? Are you ready to truly assess your wants and how that aligns with God's word? When you're ready to make this assessment, the true work can begin.

22

Let's Get Ready for Some Transparency

So, what have you been waiting, praying, dreaming, and bargaining with God about? I'm sure you can remember telling God with all sincerity "If you only grant me this one thing, I promise I won't ask for anything else!" Does that sound familiar? Well, let's be completely transparent and honest. I too have made that same confession over and over again, but the list eventually gets longer once that wish is granted. In the Word of God, we don't have to make bets with God or even try to get him to do something for us. God has given us dominion here on earth to represent him, and with that, we have the authority to declare and decree that very thing we are believing him for. In Psalms 23, God simply says, "The Lord is my shepherd; I shall not want or lack anything!"

Often times, we have prayed for things that we know we don't need in our lives, for whatever reason. Now, God does honor our prayers and wishes, but it all happens in his great timing. Have you ever just sat down and wrote out your vision on how you would want your life to be? Have you ever said to God "I want your very best for my life" even if it is not what you truly had down on paper as your vision or interest? What I came to realize even in my personal life, having several relationships, was that I never really took the time to ask God for his best for my life.

Let's look at the relationship piece for just a second. As I truly began to grow in God, the material and physical requests for a mate began to reduce and eventually disappear. As I grew, my list looked a little something like this...

- A true soulmate
- God-fearing man of God
- A hard worker
- Loyal
- Honest
- Someone who adores and loves my children as his own
- Giving
- Compassionate
- Strong, but sensitive when needed
- Bold for God

- Leader
- Family oriented
- Visionary
- A support system
- Patient

Now, we all know that patience is a big one! Patience is required to handle all of my baggage with care. By baggage, I mean my attitude, insecurities, doubts, hurts, and fears. This list could go on and on! As I started to focus on my baggage and deficiencies, the Lord spoke loudly to me, so loud I couldn't ignore it. He challenged me to cast all those issues on him and allow him to heal me inside and out so that I wouldn't have to take my future mate through those unnecessary holes of emptiness, expecting him to fill the voids. That's when I decided to just chill and dedicate consecrated time in the presence of God. I also knew that governing my life in him would allow me to shut out those things that the enemy tried to use to keep my mind on the problems and not on the true solution.

From this point, my focused totally changed. I began to get up at 5:00 a.m. to get in his presence to see what directions he had for me. During the process of what most of us call brokenness, God was only showing how much he really cared by holding my hands and holding me so very close to him. I felt Jarneen, as a person, changing daily. I could never imagine coming to a place of such peace, even while going through my last divorce. I did not allow resentment or bitterness to overcome me; instead, I let the presence of God overtake me. When I would get frustrated, God would calmly, yet strongly, bring a special peace over me. That peace was his promise to me when he told me, "Jarneen I got you." Trust me; it wasn't easy to restrain myself and not lash out. I so desperately wanted to say something ugly or just bop my husband upside the head one good time, but what was that going to do? NOTHING! The end result would have been two upset people fighting and all stirred up, once again allowing the enemy to win.

During the process of the divorce, I decided it's not when but simply how you come out of a divorce or relationship that really matters. Some might ask what I mean

26

by this statement, so let me clarify. I simply chose to walk in love and forgiveness so that my blessing would not be blocked or hindered. I prayed to God to show me myself during the process of healing so that I wouldn't contaminate my loved ones around me. Yes, it was painful and stressful at times, but God's grace was more than sufficient, and I was able to come out a winner, just as he promised I would. So, when you are facing some of the same challenges in your life, pause for a moment, take a look at your life, and immediately decide on how you want to make that final statement.

It's Personal Inventory Time

At this point, I would like to invite you to assess your personal inventory. There are several checkpoints to evaluate to make sure that you are on the right track to healing and truly seeking *His Will* for your life.

CHECKPOINT 1: *Examine your heart issues.*

By this, I mean that you must walk in forgiveness and be quick to admit if you are wrong or have missed the mark.

27

Make sure that you don't have bitterness in your heart that would cause you to do or behave outside of your character.

CHECKPOINT 2: *Stop complaining.*

Begin a self-check to make sure that you don't find yourself murmuring and complaining about certain things that you think he or should have done. It could even be a task—taking the kids to school or activities, or even whose turn it was it to cook or wash dishes. Complaining only complicates things and prolongs your healing process.

CHECKPOINT 3: *Don't sweat the petty things.*

You must learn how to pick and choose your battles. When you find yourself operating in the flesh, take a deep breath and ask God to intervene. It is very important to invite the Holy Spirit in to help us, because in our own ability when we are upset, we often don't make the best decisions. Trust that God knows how to renew our minds daily and put all your faith in him.

CHECKPOINT 4: *Be ready for change.*

Change is needed in almost every area of life when you really start to focus on *His Will* for your life. Often times, the change is concentrated on the circles in which we exist. Are your friends supportive of your change? Do they encourage you to handle your hurt in a better way or do they encourage you to act out like your old self? Yes, true change does start within, but you have to make sure that the environment around you is healthy and adaptive to your change. Would you take a shower and then put back on the same dirty clothes? No!

CHECKPOINT 5: *Have laser-sharp focus.*

Friends, stay focused, and remember that there is absolutely nothing too hard for God. Never let seemingly troubling circumstances or setbacks derail your progress. The enemy wants to trick you into thinking you must handle things your way. This is not so. Trust in His outcome of grace and you will *win*—that's what's meant by your want versus his perfect will for your life.

Assignment

Please take a moment to examine your life against the aforementioned checkpoints. Get in your quiet space, and really focus on each item to see where you fall. It also does not hurt to get feedback from a trusted and respected person who will be honest yet caring in helping you walk through this process.

Happy Assessing!

Notes & Reflections

Now that we've explored this chapter together, it's time for you to spread your wings and fly, butterfly. Use the space provided to record your notes, major takeaways, and your plan of action for moving forward. Be honest and bold! Use this quiet time to invest in YOU!

_____

_____

_____

_____

_____

_____

_____

_____

_____

_____

STEP 4: Seek and Give Pure Love, God's Kind of Love

We will start this chapter with a look at an example of love that isn't pure. I truly hope that most of you can't relate to this story, but my heart tells me that many of you will.

Joshua's Story

Joshua worked hard throughout his childhood to gain the attention and affection of his father. He always thought that if he worked harder, ran faster, got better grades, and outdid his classmates that maybe his father would want to be a part of his life. He struggled with not experiencing his father's love for many years. Through many failed efforts, Joshua never received the love he so craved.

As Joshua aged, he grew spiritually, but still craved the love of his absent father. He still longed for the day that they would be able to have a relationship. Then, out of the blue, his father called. Joshua was filled with joy at the very thought of having a conversation with his absent father. He hoped that conversation would eventually open the door to a real relationship with the man he bore a striking resemblance to, practically his twin.

Joshua began speaking to his father on a regular basis. He started feeling close to his father. He wondered if his father could actually love him one day. Maybe they finally had a

shot at truly developing a solid foundation and lifelong relationship. After just a few weeks of these frequent conversations, Joshua's father started asking for money and favors. The requests increased and made Joshua feel obligated and used. He eventually grew tired of the requests and, finally, one day said no. This angered his father, and the conversational calls eventually ceased.

Unfortunately, this was a conditional relationship with unpure motives. Joshua's father was more interested in his own gain than truly developing a relationship with his son. God's love is the exact opposite. He wants nothing from you. He simply wants to love you. How much better would this world be if we sought to bless others with this pure love, God's kind of love?

Everyone Deserves Real Love

When I began writing this chapter, the first thing that came to my spirit was unconditional love. I define unconditional love as having love for someone without having motives for gain. We all know the scripture: "For God so loved the world that he gave his only begotten son." He gave out of unselfish care for you and I. He gave his only son so that we could all be free. Can you imagine having that kind of love for someone? Could you lay down your life for your spouse, friend, or even your worst enemy? If you did, would you complain about it?

Often times, I think about how innocent a child is in life before being influenced by its environment. Children don't see color, status, or any other divisive distractions, so walking in love is very easy and normal for them. If we, as adults, still had that innocent and pure kind of love, there wouldn't be so much evil and hate in the world. We wouldn't have to experience prejudice or racism. This could only be the case if we as a people consistently demonstrated God's type of pure and unconditional love for others. As difficult as it might be for some, pure love is the only way love should be demonstrated; it's that love without motives or conditions.

Could you love someone who abandons you when they were supposedly committed to loving you? Let's be real for a moment; it's definitely more challenging to convey that same kind of unconditional love in return in the midst of pain, but that's what we are commanded to do. There is no question about it if you are a born-again believer; you are commanded to walk in love. We all want to walk in love, but it can be extremely difficult at times. Simply wanting to do it isn't

35

enough. You often have to go a step further and make a bold decision to do it. Making up your mind in advance is a premeditated, conscious choice. In doing so, your behavior, speech, and actions must line up. If you wait until you face a tough situation to decide how you want to respond, you will surely set yourself up for failure.

So, I challenge you. If there is a person whom you find very difficult to love, sow a seed of kindness or a small gift in their life. Make plans to not just put up with him or her, but go out of your way to be kind and loving to this person. Most of you might be thinking that you absolutely cannot do this, especially when that person has wronged you. You must remember, however, that you're a disciple of the Lord Jesus Christ. You are filled with his Holy Spirit and power. You must remember that God has planted in your heart his very own love, a love that never fails or waivers. So now, not only are you doing what the Word of God says, you are becoming a living witness of what pure love really is and how it is demonstrated in our daily lives.

I have learned through divorce and several failed relationships that pure and unconditional love is the only

36

righteous route; there is simply no way around it. We have to hold a high standard for others to see. If you do that, I can guarantee you that the Word of God in you will come alive!

The Holy Spirit will govern your decisions to walk in love at all times. Remember that it is not abnormal to get fed up with someone or even get to the point that you just want to tell them off. We have all been there. Even in these *human times*, the Word will speak up and remind you that love is not touchy, fretful, or resentful. So, instead of giving that person a piece of your mind, give them a piece of your heart. Give that person the love of God, and they'll be blessed. God will be pleased with your actions, and you'll have the victory of winning by displaying God's pure love!

Notes & Reflections

Now that we've explored this chapter together, it's time for you to spread your wings and fly, butterfly. Use the space provided to record your notes, major takeaways, and your plan of action for moving forward. Be honest and bold! Use this quiet time to invest in YOU!

_____

_____

_____

_____

_____

_____

_____

_____

_____

_____

_____

_____

_____

_____

_____

_____

_____

_____

_____

_____

_____

_____

_____

_____

_____

_____

STEP 5: *Realize that Forgiveness is Not a Choice....It's a Command!*

Let's test your level of forgiveness. Can you relate to Anna's story below?

Anna's Story

My friend Anna is one of the nicest people you will ever meet. She is patient and goes out of her way to help and support others. She is not quick to judge and has a magnetic personality. Anna appears to be very forgiving. She does not like conflict, but she will address issues that bother her. Once you offer an apology, Anna is quick to say, "I forgive you," and move on. That's forgiveness, right?

Well, maybe not. You see, while Anna was quick to utter the words, "I forgive you," she was often left with uneasy feelings in her spirit. We had a long conversation about this and why things seemed to revisit her in negative forms. For example, when a family member who had been very troublesome in her life died, Anna was the one person willing to forgive his past evil deeds and honor him in his passing. He was a mean man that no one else wanted to support, so Anna stepped up to the plate.

While Anna thought she had forgiven him, I would often hear her speak of the negative deposits he left in

her life. She seemed to replay his indiscretions, acknowledging how they affected her. Anna even questioned her parents about how they could let this family member do the things he did. She was willing to forgive, but not forget.

After a long conversation about what she was dealing with, Anna had a personal epiphany. She realized that her desire to get along with others harmoniously often meant that she quickly tried to move past the point of conflict so that everyone could feel comfortable. In her rush to feel comfortable, she rushed her healing process. The prayer component of forgiveness was missing in her rush to get along with others as well. We have to let the full process take place, and this involves seeking our Father so that he can properly cleanse our hearts. This is the only way true forgiveness can happen.

Forgive Or Not to Forgive—That is the Question

Throughout life, we encounter many trials that require forgiveness, both of others and ourselves. In this chapter, I want to explain the many effects (mentally, emotionally, physically, and spiritually) of unforgiveness and how to start the transformation process toward forgiveness. I want to help you discover the beauty of life without regrets and doubt.

Moving forward, I want you to be able to explore the
following:

- How to trust God's forgiveness
- Why unforgiveness takes a toll on your body,
  spirit, and mind
- How anger and regret can be replaced with
  freedom and joy
- How grace transforms thoughts, choices, and
  relationships
- The breakthrough you need to forgive yourself,
  God, and others

Does anyone really want to forgive or admit that we
need forgiveness? Who are you helping most when you
forgive the person who hurt you? YOU! That's right! You're
helping yourself more than the other person. Whether we're
giving or receiving, forgiveness is hard. I thought it seemed
so unfair for them to receive forgiveness when I had gotten
hurt. I got pain, and they got freedom without having to pay
for the pain they caused. I realized that I helped myself when
I chose to forgive. I also helped the other person by releasing

them so God can do what only He can do. If I'm in the way, trying to get revenge or take care of the situation myself, instead of trusting and obeying God, He has no obligation to deal with that person. However, God will deal with those who hurt us if we put them in His hands through forgiveness.

The act of forgiving is our seed of obedience to His Word. Once we've sown our seed, God is faithful to bring a harvest of blessing to us one way or another. Another way that forgiveness helped me is that it releases God to do His work in me. I'm happier and feel better physically when I'm not filled with the poison of unforgiveness. Serious diseases can develop as a result of the stress and pressure that bitterness, resentment, and unforgiveness put on a person. Mark 11:22-26 teaches us that unforgiveness hinders our faith from working. The Father can't forgive our sins if we don't forgive other people. We reap what we sow, my friends. Sow mercy, and you'll reap mercy; sow judgment, and you'll reap judgment. So, do yourself a favor and forgive!

There are still more benefits of forgiveness. Your fellowship with God flows freely when you're willing to forgive, but it gets blocked by unforgiveness. Forgiveness also keeps Satan from getting an advantage over us (see 2 Corinthians 2:10-11). Ephesians 4:26-27 tells us not to let the sun go down on our anger or give the devil any such foothold or opportunity. Remember that the devil must have a foothold before he can get a stronghold. Do not help Satan torture you; be quick to forgive!

Whether we're giving or receiving, forgiveness is hard. I have a few questions to help assess your ability and readiness to forgive.

1. Does your heart know how to forgive someone when trust has been broken?
2. Do you forgive just to seek harmony?
3. Once you forgive, do you truly let it go or continue to replay the ungodly deed that hurt you?
4. When your actions hurt others, do you seek forgiveness?

When someone says, "I can forgive, but I cannot forget," what he or she really is saying is, "I will not forgive." Unforgiveness, resentment, revenge, jealousy, anger, hateful attitudes, and bitterness are spiritual blockages that keep many people from living a Spirit-filled life. Keeping score of all the hurts we have suffered does more spiritual damage to us than those who have offended us. In fact, we can suffer serious physical illnesses as a result of unforgiveness.

When I was going through my divorces, I made up my mind that I was going to forgive and not carry the weight of what should have or should not have occurred in our marriage. This would only be dead weight in my heart, which could cause distress, lead to chronic health issues. Many people ruin their health and their lives by taking the poison of bitterness, resentment, and unforgiveness.

Matthew 18:23-35 tells us that if we do not forgive people, we get turned over to the torturers. It's torture to have hateful thoughts toward another person rolling around inside your head, preventing you from being able to move forward or win in every area of your life. I believe to this day that unforgiveness is a blessing blocker, and I didn't want my blessings blocked. What many women and men don't realize is that forgiveness is a key that opens the door to avenues of good health and a more satisfying life. The truth is that forgiveness blesses the giver more than it benefits the receiver. Forgiving others even when he or she did something so terrible to you or to someone you love is the unselfish act that allows God to work *His Will*. This is when the healing process begins in YOU!! Actually, you're helping yourself more than the other person. The act of forgiving is our seed of obedience to His Word. Once we've sown our seed, God is faithful to bring a harvest of blessing to us one way or another.

So, I know you're probably saying to yourself, "How do I forgive and really know I have forgiven and been forgiven?" Here are a few practical steps that must be taken.

1. DECIDE: You will never forgive if you wait until you feel like it. Choose to obey God and steadfastly resist the devil in his attempts to poison you with bitter thoughts. Make a quality decision to forgive, and God will heal your wounded emotions in due time (see Matthew 6:12-14).

2. DEPEND: You cannot forgive without the power of the Holy Spirit. It's too hard to do on your own. If '

you are truly willing, God will enable you, but you must humble yourself and cry out to Him for help. In John 20:22-23, Jesus breathed on the disciples and said, "Receive the Holy Spirit!" His next instruction was about forgiving people. Ask God to breathe the Holy Spirit on you so you can forgive those who've hurt you.

3. OBEY: Pray for your enemies and those who abuse and misuse you. Pray for their happiness and welfare (see Luke 6:27-28). Obey the Lord and watch him work in your life.

When you pray for those who have wronged you, God can and will give them the revelation that will bring them out of deception. They may not even be aware they hurt you, or maybe they're aware but are so self-centered that they don't care. When you forgive, you must cancel the debt. Do not spend your life paying and collecting debts. Hebrews 10:30 says that vengeance belongs to the Lord; He'll repay and settle the cases of His people. Forgiveness changes a life of defeat into one of victory!

47

Notes & Reflections

Now that we've explored this chapter together, it's time for you to spread your wings and fly, butterfly. Use the space provided to record your notes, major takeaways, and your plan of action for moving forward. Be honest and bold! Use this quiet time to invest in YOU!

_____

_____

_____

_____

_____

_____

_____

_____

_____

_____

STEP 6: Change Your Confessions

As you read this chapter, you will find out that what you release out of your mouth is either a result of a curse or a blessing. Words are powerful! Proverbs 18:21 states that the tongue contains the power of life and death. Thankfully, Shana learned this message before too much damage had been done.

Shana's Story

Shana was often called a complainer and worrywart, but in her mind, she was just keeping life real. She despised fakeness in people, so she was sure to always speak her truth. There was no saying she was okay just to be polite if she really wasn't. She dealt with a lot of ailments and often had to express how she was feeling. Her dysfunctional upbringing was often called into memory as she battled on a daily basis. She would tell it like it is with her family as well. She accepted her reality and didn't try to hide anything.

It was one day that I began to point out to her how she was cursing her life and overall health. I asked her why she thought she needed to confess those things as true. I had to correct my sister, in love. Her truth wasn't the sickness, ailments, or dysfunctional family. Her truth was that she was made in the perfect image of Him and his presence cannot co-exist with doubt, worry, lack, complaints, and dysfunction. You cannot invite a King to lay in filth, right? So why do we expect God to exist in negativity?

The conversation with Shana was very tough, as I did not want to offend her. It got deeper and deeper. While I seemed cool on the outside, I was nervous about addressing her confessions.

As Shana and I walked through the negative confessions that I heard her recite daily, she started to see just how negative her words were. She started to see that she was literally cursing herself, unbeknownst to her. We instantly became accountability partners in changing her confessions. She gave me permission to stop her in her tracks when she uttered negative confessions. Soon, the need for my correction decreased. I saw the shift in her; she would make a negative confession, denounce it, and restate what she was trying to say using a more positive and constructive language.

This habit does not change overnight. Shana sometimes has to correct me as well. We are both on a journey to ensure that what we confess out of our mouths aligns with the positive image we're made in. Think about it . . . God wants nothing less for us!

Now, let's focus on you and the confessions that you speak daily.

You Are What You Speak

The words you speak, whether positive or negative, will ultimately determine your quality of life. This is especially true in the area of family, relationships, career, financial decisions, and governing your family. What you release out of your mouth concerning these issues could either build you up and head you toward the path to an abundant life or push you down the road of self-destruction. I encourage you to renew your mind and begin today to speak the promises found in God's Word. God wants us to use our faith to believe and confess daily that we are the righteousness of God in Christ.

Why is this so important and how will it benefit you? Here's how. It's simple; God wants us to speak on things of excellence. This comes through your active voice, daily confessions, and praying and reading the Word. Additionally, we must learn to have a conversation with the Father. This is not a laundry list of prayers asking for things; it is having a conversation with him, just like you would with your natural parents. Most of us feel like we can talk to our parents because they are visible and easily accessible. Our Heavenly Father is easily accessible as well. I have often desired to talk to God in a way that would bring me so close to Him that I would know and feel His presence with me. As I began to put these desires into action, I learned that God also desires to hear my voice more than I could ever imagine.

God released his Word on the earth through his son Jesus Christ, not only for us to have a guide for life, but also so that we would have a means for communicating and connecting with Him, personally and intimately. It is God's desire that the full body of Christ would all speak the exact same Words, his Words, to Him with one voice and in one accord. The Bible teaches us that, out of the abundance of our hearts, the mouth speaks (Matthew 12:34).

I have gathered a list of confessions from various sources that cover every area of your life to help you build and walk in the promises that God has so beset for you. I promise you that if you apply these principles, your life will never be the same again, and you will begin to walk in victory!

Godly Confessions

Here is a list of confessions that will remind us daily of God's love and power.

I am a new creature in Christ: old things have passed away, behold, all things are new.

- 2 Corinthians 5:17 KJV

I have died and have been raised with Christ and am now seated in heavenly places.

- Ephesians 2:5-6 KJV

I am dead to sin and alive unto righteousness.

- Romans 6:11 KJV

No weapon that is formed against me shall prosper, but every tongue that rises against me in judgment, I shall show to be in the wrong.

- Isaiah 54:17

I prosper in everything I put my hand to. I have prosperity in all areas of my life—spiritually, financially, mentally, and socially.

- John 10:3-5;14-16, 27; John 14:15

I take every thought captive unto the obedience of Jesus

54

Christ, casting down every imagination, and every high and lofty thing that exalts itself against the knowledge of God.

- 2 Corinthians 10:5

As a man thinks in his heart, so is he; therefore, all of my thoughts are positive. I do not allow Satan to use my spirit as a garbage dump by meditating on negative things that he offers me.

- Proverbs 23:7 KJV

I am purposed that my mouth shall not transgress. I will speak forth the righteousness of God all the day long.

- Psalm 17:3; Psalm 35:28

I don't speak negative things.

- Ephesians 4:29

I never bind a sister or brother with the words of my mouth.

- Matthew 18:18 KJV

I am always a positive encouragement. I edify and build up; I never tear down or destroy.

- Romans 15:2

I am a believer, not a doubter.

- Mark 5:36 KJV

I am slow to speak, quick to hear, and slow to anger.

- James 1:19

I am a doer of the Word. I meditate on the Word all the day long.

- James 1:22; Psalm 1:2

I will study the Word of God. I will pray.

- 2 Timothy 2:15; Luke 18:1

I don't have a spirit of fear, but of power and love and a sound mind.

- 2 Timothy 1:7

I cast all my care on the Lord for He cares for me.

- 1 Peter 5:7 KJV

I never get tired or grow weary when I study the Word, pray, minister, or praise God; but I am alert and full of energy. And as I study, I become more alert and more energized.

- 2 Thessalonians 3:13; Isaiah 40:31

I am a giver. It is more blessed to give than to receive. I love to give! I have plenty of money to give away all the time.

- Acts 20:35; 2 Corinthians 9:7-8

I do not fear. I am not guilty.

- 1 John 4:18; Romans 8:1

I am not passive about anything, but I deal with all things in my life immediately.

- Proverbs 27:23; Ephesians 5:15-16

I do not judge my brothers and sisters in Christ Jesus after the flesh. I am a spiritual man and am judged by no one.

- John 8:15 KJV; Romans 14:10 KJV; 1 Corinthians 2:15

I have compassion and understanding for all people.

- 1 Peter 3:8

I walk in the Spirit all of the time.

- Galatians 5:16

I operate in all the gifts of the Holy Spirit, which are tongues and interpretation of tongues, the working of miracles, discerning of spirits, the word of faith, the word of knowledge, the word of wisdom, healings, and prophecy.

- 1 Corinthians 12:8-10

I have been set free. I am free to love, to worship, to trust with no fear of rejection or of being hurt.

- John 8:36; Romans 8:1

I do not hate or walk in unforgiveness.

- 1 John 2:11; Ephesians 4:32

I catch the enemy in all of his deceitful lies. I cast them down and choose rather to believe the Word of God.

- John 8:44; 2 Corinthians 2:11; 10:5 KJV

Work is good. I enjoy work!

- Ecclesiastes 5:19

I do all my work excellently and with great prudence—making the most of all of my time.

- Ecclesiastes 9:10; Proverbs 22:29; Ephesians 5:15-16

I am a responsible person. I enjoy responsibility, and I rise to every responsibility in Jesus.

- 2 Corinthians 11:28 KJV; Philippians 4:13

I am creative because the Holy Spirit lives in me.

- John 14:26; 1 Corinthians 6:19

I take good care of my body. I eat right, I look good, I feel good, and I weigh what God wants me to weigh.

- 1 Corinthians 9:27; 1 Timothy 4:8 TLB

Pain cannot successfully come against my body because Jesus bore all my pain.

- Isaiah 53:3-4

I lay hands on the sick, and they recover.

- Mark 16:18

I have a teachable spirit.

- 2 Timothy 2:24 KJV

I do not think more highly of myself than I ought to in the flesh.

- Romans 12:3

I have humbled myself, and God has exalted me.

- 1 Peter 5:6 KJV

I do what I say I will do, and I get where I am going on time.

- Luke 16:10; 2 Peter 3:14 KJV

All my household are blessed in their deeds: we're blessed when we come in and when we go out.

- Deuteronomy 28:6 KJV

I don't hurry and rush; I do one thing at a time.

- Proverbs 19:2; 21:5

All that I own is paid for. I owe no man anything except to love him in Christ.

- Romans 13:8

I am anointed of God for ministry.

- Luke 4:18

I am an obedient wife, and no rebellion operates in me.

- Ephesians 5:22,24 TLB; 1 Samuel 15:23 KJV

My husband is wise. He is the king and priest of our home. He makes godly decisions.

- Proverbs 31:10-12; Revelation 1:6 KJV; Proverbs 21:1

All my children have lots of Christian friends, and God has set aside a Christian wife or husband for each of them.

- 1 Corinthians 15:33

My children love to pray and study the Word. They openly and boldly praise God.

- 2 Timothy 2:15

Friends, you are what you speak. Let's work together to get in the positive habit of changing our confessions and watch the change that takes place in your life. Watch God honor your efforts. You will see the manifestation of love, strength, and power in your life.

As you change your confessions, be sure to go into a protective space and don't allow others to speak negative confessions over your life. I often hear people laugh in agreement as their friends and family playfully call them names. Lack of correction is agreement, and that becomes another confession that you have allowed in your spirit. A part of this process has to involve the gentle correction of others that speak these negative confessions into your life.

Let's start today. Change your thoughts and words, and change your life!

Notes & Reflections

Now that we've explored this chapter together, it's time for you to spread your wings and fly, butterfly. Use the space provided to record your notes, major takeaways, and your plan of action for moving forward. Be honest and bold! Use this quiet time to invest in YOU!

_____

_____

_____

_____

_____

_____

_____

_____

_____

_____

_____

_____

_____

_____

_____

_____

STEP 7: Realize that He Created You to Be "Unapologetically Me"

Let's look at Rochelle's testimony. I think this will help a lot of you.

Rochelle's Story

Rochelle was a faithful servant at her local church. She actively volunteered in ministry and spent much of her free time there. After serving in church for a while, Rochelle became aware of implied standards for parishioners and church leaders. These standards went well past the expressed biblical standards; they were more like standards that weren't necessarily addressed in the Bible. For example, as a person serving in ministry, she was asked to say "My pleasure" instead of "No problem" or "Sure thing" while responding to a "thanks" from another church member. She was often told how to think, talk, dress, and even how to relate to others through her ministry involvement.

Slowly but surely, Rochelle felt herself turning into a woman she no longer recognized. She was once a fiery, quick-witted, and outspoken woman but that seemed to disappear the longer she stayed in ministry. The unique characteristics she was born with became consumed by the robot she was becoming. She no longer felt her own spark.

64

Was this of God? How could it be? She no longer liked herself. Was this what God truly wanted for her life? She struggled with this for at least 2 years before she finally received her answer. Rochelle heard God in her quiet time. This time started with a stroll down the memory lane. She remembered the person she was and quickly started to assess the person she had become, and she didn't like what she saw. God quickly swept in and reaffirmed her! In this time, he spoke to her heart and told her that he called her to ministry as an example to others. Not a manufactured example to others, but a true example of God's love through real people. Not pretentious people who seemed unapproachable to the common unbeliever. At that moment, Rochelle finally understood that she didn't have to stop being herself to serve God and to love him. He accepted her quick wit, silly personality, and loud mouth. He created her with these qualities because her livelihood would be infectious to people that didn't know Him. Through her, they would see the fullness of God and how fun and unrestrictive submission to Him can really be!

I Just Want to Be Me

Often times, we try hard to fit into the box that others place us in. This box is often restrictive and limits our natural ability to be the person God has called us to be! Why would we allow someone to compartmentalize who we are and what we are capable of doing? This is often the result of cultural conditioning. We are conditioned to go with the flow and to act properly, as to not offend others. This conditioning can cause us to follow the status quo in hopes of simply getting along with others. Let's face it; no one wants to be labeled as the "troublemaker" or "problem child," right? We were raised better than that! We were raised to be respectful, God-fearing men and women! How dare you not conform to the limited space someone tries to trap you in! How dare you not agree with someone else's perception of who you are, who you should be, and what you should be doing with your life?

When you write this concept out, it seems asinine, right? It's really not though. Think about it. Most of us live our lives trying to live up to someone else's standards. It might be our parents, siblings, boss, friends, or society as a whole. It might even be your church family. Oh yes, I said it! Church family, as referenced in Rochelle's story. No matter the orchestrator of the box people want to put you in, the fact is that people will conveniently place you in the box they create if you allow them to. We can all learn from Rochelle's story. She spent so much time trying to conform to a standard that God didn't set for her. It was only after truly hearing God's desire for her life that she began to understand who she is in God and embrace the fierce warrior God called her to be! God didn't want her to be a quiet and meek "yes" girl. He wanted her to remain funny, exciting, loud, and infectious! After all, He created her and gave her these characteristics. God calls us because of our uniqueness. He doesn't call us to act like everyone else in the kingdom. Can you imagine how boring that would be? How are we to be of witness to others, without our own unique flare?

The important thing to remember here is God made you. He is responsible for the person you became, flaws and all. He doesn't want you to pretend to be someone you are not. He simply wants you to be you while living a life that is pleasing to Him. Be yourself and never allow someone to put you in their box—you will never fit! Follow God's plan for your life, offering no apologies when people don't understand or agree with that plan.

Other people's agreement with God's plan for your life is irrelevant. Even as adults, peer pressure is still a factor in our lives. We can be pressured into trying to fit in with co-workers, sorority and fraternity organizations, church organizations or any other important affiliations. We must remain steadfast and be true to ourselves. So, I challenge you to embrace who you are and make no apologies for it; be unapologetically YOU!!

Accept my challenge and reinforce the new YOU by meditating on these awesome quotes found in Steve Maraboli's *Unapologetically You: Reflections on Life and the Human Experience.*

"If you hang out with chickens, you're going to cluck and if you hang out with eagles, you're going to fly."

"We all make mistakes, have struggles, and even regret things in our past, but you are not your mistakes, you are not your struggles, and you are here NOW with the power to shape your day and your future; hold steadfast."

"The truth is, unless you let go, unless you forgive yourself, unless you forgive the situation, unless you realize that the situation is over, you absolutely cannot move forward."

"There is nothing more rare, nor more beautiful, than a woman being unapologetically herself; comfortable in her perfect imperfection. That is the true essence of beauty."

"When in a relationship, a real man doesn't make his woman jealous of others; he makes others jealous of his woman."

"I will not try to convince you to love me, to respect me, to commit to me. I deserve better than that; I AM BETTER THAN THAT...Goodbye."

"We all make mistakes, have struggles, and even regret things in our past. But you are not your mistakes, you are not your struggles, and you are here NOW with the power to shape your day and your future; walk in it boldly, my friend."

"Renew, release, let go. Yesterday's gone. There's nothing you can do to bring it back. You can't *should've* done something. You can only DO something. Renew yourself. Release that attachment. Today is a beautiful new day!"

"Live your truth. Express your love. Share your enthusiasm. Take action towards your dreams. Walk your talk. Dance and sing to your music. Embrace your blessings. Make today worth remembering."

"I find the best way to love someone is not to change them, but instead, help them reveal the greatest version of themselves."

"People tend to be generous when sharing their nonsense, fear, and ignorance. And while they seem quite eager to feed you their negativity, please remember that sometimes the diet we need to be on is a spiritual and emotional one. Be cautious with what you feed your mind and soul. Fuel yourself with positivity and let that fuel propel you into positive action."

"The reason many people in our society are miserable, sick, and highly stressed is because of an unhealthy attachment to things they have no control over."

"I promise you nothing is as chaotic as it seems. Nothing is worth diminishing your health. Nothing is worth poisoning yourself into stress, anxiety, and fear."

"Your complaints, your drama, your victim mentality, your whining, your blaming, and all of your excuses have NEVER gotten you even a single step closer to your goals or dreams. Let go of your nonsense. Let go of the delusion that you DESERVE better and go EARN it! Today is a new day!"

"There is great change to be experienced once you learn the power of letting go. Stop allowing anyone or anything to control, limit, repress, or discourage you from being your true self! Today is YOURS to shape [—] own it [—] break free from people and things that poison or dilute your spirit."

In Closing, Remember This...

"There is nothing more beautiful than seeing a person being themselves. Imagine the beauty of going through your day being unapologetically you."

This ends our time together, for now. I truly hope this book has blessed you and encouraged you to come from behind the curtain to reveal the true essence of YOU!

With Love,

Jarneen

Notes & Reflections

Now that we've explored this chapter together, it's time for you to spread your wings and fly, butterfly. Use the space provided to record your notes, major takeaways, and your plan of action for moving forward. Be honest and bold! Use this quiet time to invest in YOU!

_____

_____

_____

_____

_____

_____

_____

_____

_____